5077

WINDOWS OF GRACE
A TRIBUTE OF LOVE

THE MEMORIAL WINDOWS OF
ST. PAUL'S EPISCOPAL CHURCH
RICHMOND, VIRGINIA

CONTENTS

WINDOW	LOCATION	MAKER	PAGE
Introduction			3
Schematic Plan of Window Locations			7
EAST AISLE (From Back to Front of Sanctuary)			
Newton-Davenport Window	LE1	Tiffany Studios	8
Newton-Davenport Window	UE1	Tiffany Studios	10
Blair Window	LE2	Tiffany Studios	12
John Brooke Young Window	UE2	Louis C. Tiffany (Tiffany Studios)	14
Lee Memorial Window (lower)	LE3	Henry Holiday	16
Lee Memorial Window (upper)	UE3	Henry Holiday	18
Joseph Reid Anderson Window	LE4	Tiffany Studios	20
John Langbourne Williams Window	UE4	Lamb Studios	22
Griffin B. Davenport Window	LE5	Heaton, Butler & Bayne*	24
Ella de Treville Window	UE5	Tiffany Studios	26
CHANCEL			
William Hamilton Macfarland Window	A1	Lavers & Westlake*	28
Elizabeth Mayo Ross Window	A2	Lavers & Westlake*	30
Joseph Reid Anderson Altarpiece		Tiffany Studios	32
Sarah Eliza Anderson Window	A3	Lavers & Westlake*	34
Pegram Window	A4	Lavers & Westlake*	36
George Woodbridge Window	A5	H.W. Jenkins & Son	38
WEST AISLE (From Front to Back of Sanctuary)			
John Marshall Window	LW5	Lamb Studios	40
John Brockenbrough Newton Window	UW5	Tiffany Studios	42
Haxall Window	LW4	Charles Booth Studio	44
Strother-Buford Window	UW4	Tiffany Studios	46
Jefferson Davis Window (lower)	LW3	Tiffany Studios	48
Jefferson Davis Window (upper)	UW3	Tiffany Studios	50
Charles Macgill Window	LW2	Silas McBee/Charles Booth Studio	52
Macgill-Swan Window	UW2	Silas McBee/Charles Booth Studio	54
Richard L. Maury and Matthew F. Maury Window	LW1	Gorham Manufacturing Company	56
Susan E. Maury Window	UW1	Gorham Manufacturing Company	58
CHAPEL WINDOWS			
Marie and Kate Gerdy Window	C1	Franz Mayer Co., Munich	60
Fanny Braxton Young Miller Window	C2	Franz Mayer Co., Munich	61
Marie Cooke Hickey and James J. Hickey Window	C3	Franz Mayer Co., Munich	62
Acknowledgments			63
Sponsors and Contributors			64

*Attributed to

INTRODUCTION

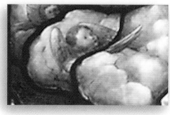

The stained-glass windows of St. Paul's are familiar and much-loved fixtures of our church. Most of the windows have been in place for a hundred years or more. The windows' many figures are old friends who greet us at every service. They include angels, saints, prophets, disciples, and apostles. We have at least eighteen depictions of Christ. We also have images of ordinary people: children, troubled people, astonished people, and crowds of people, a crowd of over 100 in one window alone. But the windows show some not-so-pleasant people too, including Pharaoh and his attendants, as well as Bernice, sister of King Herod Agrippa and mistress of the Emperor Titus. We also have in our windows a bountiful display of flowers and other plants: madonna lilies, lilies of the valley, morning glories, roses, daisies, hyssop, anemones, ferns, palms, laurel, and a host of fruits are all found here. Especially entrancing, however, is the display of weather patterns as seen in the windows' variety of cloud formations: stormy clouds, billowy clouds, pink sunrise clouds, golden sunset clouds, heavenly blue clouds, misty clouds, and iridescent clouds.

As much as anything, the windows are treasured works of art. Their glowing hues and moving compositions enhance the beauty of the church. The names of some of the most prominent stained-glass artisans of both England and America are represented. Foremost among them is the celebrated Louis Comfort Tiffany, whose studios have provided us ten windows and one mosaic Other leading artisans whose work we see include the

English maker Henry Holiday, Lavers & Westlake of London, Lamb Studios, the Gorham Manufacturing Company, the Charles Booth Studio, Franz Mayer of Munich, and the London studio of Heaton, Butler & Bayne. Despite their diversity in style, color, and technique, the windows are surprisingly compatible with one another.

The windows also tell stories. Beginning in the Middle Ages, a primary function of stained-glass windows was to portray Biblical stories or to convey religious lessons to largely illiterate worshippers. St. Paul's windows continue the tradition of presenting stories and lessons. We see depictions of famous Biblical events such as the Annunciation, the visit of the Magi, the Resurrection, the Ascension, Jesus among the Temple elders, and

Jesus raising the young man at Nain. We see figurative representations of religious virtues: the Kiss of Charity, the Angel of Hope, the angels of Goodness and Mercy, and the young crusader. Moreover, we see portraits of Biblical personages: Moses, St. Paul, Cornelius, King Herod Agrippa, and Cleopas.

We need to remember that St. Paul's windows are memorials as well. As such, the windows are constant reminders of former parishioners and other individuals who have contributed to the life of the church, and whose deaths were mourned. Some of those honored have achieved great fame: Jefferson Davis, Robert E. Lee, John Marshall, and Joseph Reid Anderson are principal luminaries. Others are remembered as loved parents, a lost spouse, or mourned children. One window honors a boy scout who died aiding people in the influenza pandemic of 1918. Together, the many individuals honored by the windows are part of the rich fabric of the church's history. The windows help keep their names alive to us.

As originally designed in the early 1840s, St. Paul's was one of the country's purest examples of the Greek Revival style. Its architect, Thomas S. Stewart of Philadelphia, did not intend the church to have stained-glass windows. We recall that from the late seventeenth century through the mid-nineteenth century, the Anglican Church, and subsequently the American Episcopal Church, was

decidedly Protestant in its practices. Religious images and symbols were associated with Roman Catholicism, and were eschewed by the Church of England. Indeed, eighteenth-century Anglican churches in both England and America were essentially devoid of religious iconography; their windows were nearly always clear glass. Images of Christ, the Virgin Mary, and other religious figures, whether in stained glass, sculpture, or architectural ornament, were discouraged if not

forbidden. St. Paul's continued in that tradition. When the church was consecrated in 1845, the only religious symbol worked into the fabric of its architecture was the tetragrammaton, a triangle containing the four Hebrew letters of Yahweh, or Jehovah, in the central ceiling medallion. If St. Paul's displayed a cross, it was nothing more than a small portable cross placed on the Holy Table (never referred to as an altar) during services. The rest of the architectural decoration consisted of Classical Greek ornaments. In keeping with the style of the times, our first windows were all clear glass, which flooded the interior with daylight.

The revival of the use of stained glass in Anglican churches, including American Episcopal churches, came about through the influence of the ecclesiological movement. This was a movement that arose in England in the 1840s as an effort to revive medieval art and architecture in the Church. It was the aim of the movement's advocates, the Ecclesiologists, to play down the Protestant aspect of the Anglican Church and return to it the splendor of its medieval heritage. Not only did they promote the Gothic style for church architecture, they also encouraged the use of the rich colors and elaborate ritual of the medieval liturgy. In particular, they revived the art and craft of religious stained glass, an essential fixture of Gothic-style churches. American Episcopalians followed suit. Throughout the country scores of ecclesiologically correct Gothic-style or Gothic Revival churches, replete with medieval-style stained-glass windows, sprang up. But not just new Gothic Revival churches were outfitted with stained glass; many older churches, wanting to keep up with fashion, went about replacing their clear windows with stained glass.

The ecclesiological movement touched St. Paul's in 1890 with the deepening of its chancel, an effort to help the church accommodate the new, more complex, liturgical forms promoted by the Ecclesiologists. This architectural alteration resulted in the removal of the church's very Protestant center pulpit, and the installation of an altar, embellished in 1896 with Tiffany's mosaic of Leonardo da Vinci's Last Supper. A key element of the project was the placement of four memorial windows in the newly reconfigured chancel. While church records do not record the maker of these windows, Peter Cormack, Acting Keeper of the William Morris Gallery in London, has attributed them to Lavers & Westlake, a prominent London firm. Because England was a leader in stained-glass manufactory, it was not unusual for many late 19th-century American churches to be outfitted with English works.

The chancel windows may be the first stained-glass windows installed in St. Paul's, but they were not the first considered. The vestry minutes record that in 1889, a committee was appointed to seek the acquisition of "two conspicuous windows to be dedicated as memorial windows to perpetuate the names of Robert E. Lee and Jefferson Davis." The upper and lower Lee windows were received in 1892, but Tiffany's windows honoring Jefferson Davis were not installed until 1898. Between 1890 and 1912, however, the majority of St. Paul's original clear glass windows were replaced with stained glass, resulting in a dramatic change to the character of the interior. Two more windows, the John Langbourne Williams window, and the John Brooke Young window, were not installed until the mid-1920s. The latter is an unusually late example of Tiffany glass. Thus, by the late 1920s, all but two of the church's windows were filled with stained glass. The vestry decreed that the original windows in the rear, including those on either side of the organ case, should stay unchanged as a reminder of the church's early character.

The three windows in St. Paul's chapel were dedicated in 1936 and 1937. The chapel, located immediately below the chancel, is a space originally used as the vestry meeting room. The windows

were designed and crafted by the celebrated firm of Franz Mayer of Munich, founded in 1847. These windows are our best examples of medieval-style stained glass, similar to what is seen in French cathedrals.

Just over a century from the time St. Paul's first considered installing stained glass, the parish became the fortunate recipient of three more windows, through the generosity of the Historic Richmond Foundation. The windows were formerly in Monumental Church, the 1814 masterpiece of architect Robert Mills. The church's owner, the Historic Richmond Foundation, was undertaking a long-term restoration of the church, a project that included the reconstruction of the original clear-glass windows. It needed to find appropriate homes for its six memorial windows. The foundation thus divided them between St. Paul's and St. James's, the two parishes that traced their ancestry to Monumental. St. Paul's needed additional windows to fill the three voids created when its chancel organ was removed and replaced by the new Rosales organ in the rear gallery. The three Monumental Church windows, installed in 1998, consist of a Lamb Studios window

DETAILS TOP TO BOTTOM:
GRIFFIN B. DAVENPORT WINDOW
UPPER LEE MEMORIAL WINDOW
JOHN LANGBOURNE WILLIAMS
    WINDOW
CHARLES MACGILL WINDOW

honoring U.S. Supreme Court Chief Justice John Marshall, a Tiffany window honoring Bishop John Brockenbrough Newton, and an H.W. Jenkins and Sons window in memory of the Rev. George Woodbridge. The Woodbridge window, dating from 1879, is the oldest window in St. Paul's. Because they are not on an outside wall, all three windows have to be artificially lighted.

In the late 1990s, St. Paul's initiated a continuing program of conservation of all its stained glass. Some of the windows are in relatively good condition, and can merely be cleaned in place. Others have considerable structural fatigue, and have had to be completely removed, disassembled, and releaded–a process that sometimes takes several months for an individual window. Careful dismantling is required of all the Tiffany windows, as dirt penetrates the windows' several layers. Each layer has to separated, cleaned, and reattached.

The conservation program is a formal commitment by St. Paul's parish to the stewardship of its artistic treasures. It is hoped that this book, with its numerous illustrations as well as a short history and description of each window, will engender a deeper appreciation of this special legacy–one that has enriched our worship and one that we hope will nourish the eye and soul of all who enter our church.

Schematic Plan of Window Locations

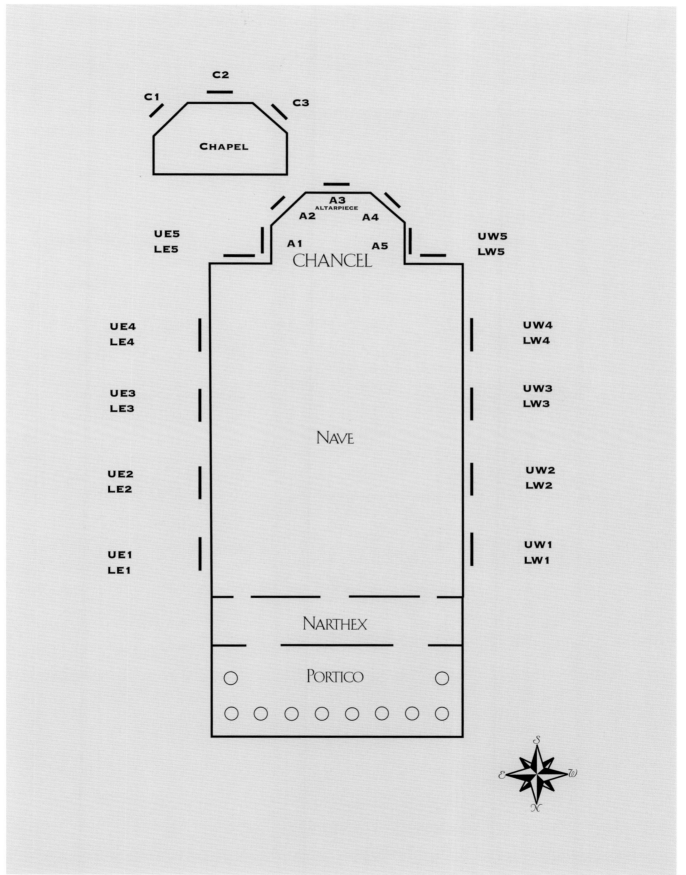

Newton-Davenport Window

Tiffany Studios
Installed ca. 1901

*Dedicated to the memory of Mary Heath Newton (1852-1899)
and Eliza Nye Allen Davenport (1819-1889) and Isaac
Davenport, Jr. (1815-1896) Donated by Virginius Newton,
husband of Mary Heath Davenport Newton*

The Annunciation

The pair of windows given by Virginius Newton, a former Confederate naval officer and later a distinguished Richmond citizen, form one of St. Paul's treasures. The principal window of the two, the lower one, depicts the Annunciation. Here, the Archangel Gabriel appears to announce to Mary that she has found favor with God and shall conceive a child whom she is to name Jesus.

Tiffany's portrayal of Gabriel follows conventional representations. Gabriel's left hand is held high in a gesture of salutation. He wears a crown and holds a scepter, both objects serving as symbols of his divine authority. Consistent with other traditional depictions of Gabriel, his wings are large and multicolored. Mary is also shown following accepted conventions. She is kneeling at a low table, having been interrupted from reading the book on the table surface. At the lower left is a vase of lilies, both a symbol of Mary's purity and an attribute of Gabriel. Above Mary is the dove of the Holy Spirit casting its radiance upon her.

The composition is rendered almost entirely in tones of blue and silver blended with gold. The work is a triumph in what Tiffany described as "Favrile" glass, a principal product of his studio. The term is derived from the Latin "fabrile," meaning handcrafted. With his Favrile glass Tiffany provides here lustrous effects of iridescent light, its inner glows ever changing as the sun changes positions. Two focal points of the composition are the faces of Mary and Gabriel. Like most of Tiffany's faces, they are carefully painted. Mary's face is a memorable portrayal of the purity of feminine beauty. Her downcast eye has particular delicacy.

Newton-Davenport Window

TIFFANY STUDIOS
INSTALLED CA. 1901

*Dedicated to the memory of Mary Heath Davenport Newton
(1852-1899) and Eliza Nye Allen Davenport (1819-1889) and
Isaac Davenport, Jr. (1815-1896)
Donated by Virginius Newton,
husband of Mary Heath Davenport Newton*

The Fruit of the Spirit

Louis Comfort Tiffany's stained-glass windows have a unique character. The absence of comparable work by other studios makes his windows immediately recognizable. Tiffany was always experimenting; he mixed various chemicals and tried different firing techniques to achieve new effects with glass. Some of his efforts were failures; others resulted in gorgeous textures of iridescent color that Tiffany exploited and incorporated into his studio's products. Because much of his output was the result of improvisation, his many works were essentially immune from imitation by other glassmakers.

Many of Tiffany's special touches are evident in the upper section of the Newton-Davenport window. Here, the silvery, multi-layered glass makes billowy clouds, misty blue sky, lustrous angel feathers, and diaphanous robes. For the robes Tiffany employed "drapery" or "ribbon" glass, where the cooling molten glass was pulled to create actual three-dimensional waves imitating folds of cloth.

This upper window is a celebration of the Annunciation, the subject of its companion window below. Four angels make joyful noise on their musical instruments: cymbals, strings, pipes, and flute. The window's inscription signals the message of the Annunciation: "The Fruit of the Spirit is Love, Peace, Gentleness, Goodness, Faith." Through the swirling patterns of the lead cames, one can almost hear the angels' music.

As with all Tiffany windows, the forms and coloring come primarily from the manipulation of the opalescent glass, the exception being the angels' faces and hands, which are painted. Tiffany used models for his faces, which explains why similar likenesses can be found in different windows. The classic beauty of the faces here, however, makes it difficult to believe that the images are not idealized. The single star in the clouds symbolizes the Virgin's title "Stella Maris," Star of the Sea.

BLAIR WINDOW

TIFFANY STUDIOS
INSTALLED 1896

*Dedicated to the memories of Adolphus Blair (1843-1893) and
his wife, Ellen Beirne Blair (1848-1875)
Donated by the Blair children*

TO THE GLORY OF GOD AND SACRED TO THE MEMORIES OF
ADOLPHUS BLAIR AND HIS WIFE ELLEN BEIRNE BLAIR
ERECTED BY THEIR CHILDREN

THE VISION OF CHRIST TO BELIEVERS

The Blair window belongs to St. Paul's highly significant collection of eleven Tiffany works, including the mosaic altarpiece. Its subject is the vision of the risen Christ to believers, a scene that vividly reveals Christ's divinity.

The ascended Jesus and attendant angels are shown as translucent apparitions. Jesus wears a cassock of shimmering white, white being symbolic of purity and holiness of life. White also was the color described as being worn by Jesus after his resurrection. Jesus' face is the image of physical perfection, and is given an expression of beatific calm. The presence of angels to each side of him further reinforces this revelation of Jesus as a holy being. Like Jesus, the angels wear white cassocks, their heads framed by halos, auras of light edged with gold. Their halos differ from Jesus' halo, which is a gold ring encircling a plain cross, an acknowledgment of his triumph over crucifixion. The angels' hands are pressed together in prayer. By contrast, Jesus' arms are held down in an attitude of salutation, with his left hand making the sign of the Trinity.

Kneeling at Jesus' feet are two pilgrims, awed by the ethereal scene before them. One holds a lamp, recalling the Biblical description of the Word of God as a lamp to the faithful. The other has set his lamp on the ground while lifting his hands in prayer.

Adolphus Blair, who is honored by this window, was regarded by Richmonders as a citizen of exceptional Christian virtue. He served on St. Paul's vestry and for many years was church register. The vestry's resolution adopted at his death stated: "Not only was he the very heart and soul of the spiritual and practical work of St. Paul's—its Sabbath School, its Church Homes, its Charity Chapter—but he was also the founder and father of the mission which has developed into St. Andrew's Church."

JOHN BROOKE YOUNG WINDOW

LOUIS C. TIFFANY (TIFFANY STUDIOS)
INSTALLED BETWEEN 1925 AND 1928

*Dedicated to the memory of
John Brooke Young (1861-1924)
Donated by Anne Gray Young,
widow of John Brooke Young*

CORNELIUS AND THE ANGEL

Signed "Louis C. Tiffany, N.Y.," this representation of the visit of an angel to the Roman centurion, Cornelius, is a late example of the work of the Tiffany Studios. Cornelius is regarded as the first Gentile to convert to Christianity. As recounted in the Book of Acts, Cornelius is described as a monotheist, a devout God-fearing person. While he was praying one day, an angel appeared to him, telling him to dispatch men to Joppa to bring Peter to him. Peter was duly brought to Cornelius. After Peter preached, the Holy Spirit fell upon the both of them and they began to speak in tongues as at Pentecost.

Peter told Cornelius and his family that God shows no partiality, and that Jesus is Lord of all. Cornelius and his family immediately converted to Christianity. Peter then baptized them. This occasion, of profound importance to early Christian history, symbolically represented the admission of Gentiles to full and equal fellowship with Jewish Christians. It marked the first fruit of Christ's command to the disciples, as recorded in Matthew, to go and make disciples of all nations.

In this window the angel appears out of blue clouds, holding its hand up in a gesture of greeting. Cornelius is shown in Roman uniform, but holding a heavy gold cross in one arm. His face has the stern features of a martial leader. The angel grasps a luminous palm branch, an object that holds a double meaning. Originally, the palm branch was a symbol of military victory, carried in triumphal processions. It was adopted by the early Church as a symbol of Christians' victory over sin and death.

John Brooke Young served on St. Paul's vestry for thirty years and was greatly admired by the parish for his kindly and courteous manner. A testimonial passed by the vestry stated: "He had been ever faithful in his attendance, and cheerful in the performance of every duty assigned to him."

Lee Memorial Window (Lower)

Henry Holiday, artist and maker
Installed 1892

Dedicated to the memory of Robert Edward Lee (1807-1870)
Donated by Annie Carter Stewart, Lucy Norma Stewart, and
Elizabeth Hope Stewart

Moses Leaving the House of Pharaoh

The pair of windows honoring Robert E. Lee was the gift of three maiden daughters of John and Amanda Stewart. Plans for windows dedicated to General Lee were in progress as early as 1889. From the beginning, it was intended to place them opposite pew 111, the pew occupied by Lee and his family during the Civil War and afterwards. The windows were executed by the famed English stained-glass artist, Henry Holiday, who visited America in 1890, where he was a guest at Brook Hill, the Stewarts' Henrico County estate. There Holiday learned about Lee's life and character, and developed the windows' designs.

Holiday, along with his colleagues Edward Burne-Jones and Dante Gabriel Rossetti, belonged to the artistic movement known as the Pre-Raphaelites, whose influence can be seen in the bold facial profiles of the window's figures. The composition follows the inscription: "By Faith Moses refused to be called the Son of Pharaoh's Daughter; Choosing rather to suffer affliction with the Children of God. For he Endured as seeing Him who is invisible." This subject alludes to Robert E. Lee's decision to refuse the offer of command of the Union forces, and to ally himself with his native Virginians and the Confederacy. Indeed, the figure of Moses bears a resemblance to Lee as a young military officer.

The scene shows Moses, the image of manly perfection, in the attire of a prince, turning away from the house of Pharaoh and dropping his wand of office. Pharaoh's daughter and her handmaidens, gorgeously appareled beneath the ceremonial peacock fan, stand by. Above, Pharaoh sits sphinx-like on a royal barge among his attendants. Scattered through the window is an array of Egyptian motifs, including hieroglyphs on the wall surfaces. Holiday produced a near-identical window for England's Durham Cathedral in 1895.

LEE MEMORIAL WINDOW (UPPER)

HENRY HOLIDAY, ARTIST AND MAKER
INSTALLED 1892

Dedicated to the memory of Robert Edward Lee (1807-1870)
Donated by Annie Carter Stewart, Lucy Norma Stewart, and
Elizabeth Hope Stewart

MOSES ON MOUNT NEBO

The upper section of St. Paul's famed pair of Henry Holiday windows honoring Robert E. Lee is a depiction of Moses on Mount Nebo. This is where God allowed Moses to view the Promised Land shortly before he died. In contrast to the image of the young Moses in the window below, Moses is seen here as a bearded old man, resembling Lee's appearance at the end of the Civil War. A focal point of the composition is Moses' beautifully modeled hand pointing heavenward. The pair of angels, God's messengers, hold a continuous scroll bearing the words: "The eternal God is thy refuge and underneath are the everlasting arms". The pathway to the mountain top is shown as a golden cloud.

A striking feature of this window is the sea of faces in the lower area, representing the Children of Israel, grouped before their tents on the plains of Moab. As described by Elizabeth Weddell in her 1931 history of St. Paul's Church: "They stand silent, motionless, and overawed, awaiting the return of their leader after his vigil with his Maker on the remote mountain top." While it is difficult to separate them out, there may be as many as 100 people shown in this remarkable scene. The Book of Deuteronomy says that following his death, the people of Israel wept for Moses on the plains of Moab for thirty days.

Holiday's window is a vivid contrast to the upper section of Tiffany's Jefferson Davis memorial window on the wall opposite. Instead of Tiffany's vaporous luminescence, Holiday employs the richest of color palettes: emerald greens, sapphire blues, and both ruby and rose reds. Moses' blue robe sets him off as the dominant figure of the composition. The green blanket draped over him may allude to the tradition of green being a symbol of victory and hope for immortality.

JOSEPH REID ANDERSON WINDOW

TIFFANY STUDIOS
INSTALLED 1894

Dedicated to the memory of Joseph Reid Anderson (1813-1892)
Donated by Joseph Reid Anderson's family

JESUS BLESSING THE CHILDREN

This classic example of Tiffany artistry was given by the family of Joseph Reid Anderson, a vestryman of St. Paul's for forty-eight years and senior warden for twenty years. Anderson is best known for his service to the Confederacy. He was appointed a brigadier general in 1861, but the following year Confederate authorities asked him to be the director of Richmond's Tredegar Iron Works, which Anderson had led before the war. Tredegar became the chief manufacturer of armaments for the Southern forces. General Anderson continued as Tredegar's president after the war and held the office until his death in 1892.

The focus of the Anderson window, children, is signaled by the inscription: "Blessed are the Pure in Heart, for they shall see God" (Matthew 5: 8). Children are symbols of purity and innocence. Here, Jesus holds one in his arm and rests his hand on the head of another, a reminder of his admonition to his disciples to let the little children come to him–"for to such belongs the kingdom of God" (Luke 18: 16). The children's faces are wonderfully tender, especially that of the infant peacefully asleep on Jesus' shoulder. Their mothers watch with expressions of calm and trust. The women's chiseled features and sensual mouths conform to standards of feminine beauty of the 1890s.

Tiffany's mastery of color is evident in Jesus' radiant red garment, a symbol of majesty. His divine status is highlighted by the luminous gold arch, suggestive of a halo. Within the arch is an ethereal cloudscape formed by a melding of golds and blues in the glass. The window's colors, long muted by dirt that had penetrated the various layers of glass, were restored to their original brilliance following conservation in 2002-03. They are especially vivid when illuminated by the morning sun.

John Langbourne Williams Window

LAMB STUDIOS
INSTALLED 1928

Dedicated to the memory of
John Langbourne Williams (1903-1918)
Donated by Mr. and Mrs. Edmund Randolph Williams,
parents of John Langbourne Williams

The Young Crusader

John Langbourne Williams, known as Jack to his family, was the son of Edmund Randolph and Maude Stokes Williams. He died at age fifteen during the influenza pandemic of 1918, having contracted the fatal disease helping the sick and dying as a member of the Richmond Boy Scouts ambulance corps. The pandemic, one of modern history's greatest health disasters, infected twenty-eight per cent of the American population, and killed between 20 and 40 million people worldwide.

The nobility of Jack's self-sacrifice is symbolized in this window by a youthful crusader kneeling before an angel who blesses him with a crown of laurel leaves, a symbol of glory. The angel, with its beatific expression, appears weightless, its bare feet floating just above the ground. The angel's robe has the translucent shimmer of mother-of-pearl. The bowed head of the young knight, seen only from behind, emphasizes the fact that the window honors one struck down in the prime of life. On the knight's tabard is a red cross, a mark of valiant service. The window's theme is highlighted by the inscription: "Greater love hath no man than this that he lay down his life for his friend." Worked into the design of the lower corners, are the insignia of the Boy Scouts, with the scout motto: "Be Prepared."

Lamb Studios, maker of the window, was founded in 1857, and is the oldest continuously operating stained glass studio in the United States. Lamb Studios windows of this period are similar in their pictorial style to Tiffany Studios windows but employ a stronger, less luminous, color palette. In this window, the composition is dominated by the rich greens of the landscape setting. The Williams window is one of two Lamb Studios windows in St. Paul's.

GRIFFIN B. DAVENPORT WINDOW

Dedicated to the memory of
Griffin Barney Davenport (1824-1889)
Donated by the Davenport family

JESUS HEALING THE SICK

This richly detailed window, with its jewel-like colors, forms a backdrop for the church's baptismal font. Its subject is Jesus healing the sick, with the inscription: "Come Unto Me All Ye That Labour And Are Heavy Laden And I Will Give You Rest" (Matthew 11:28).

Jesus appears outside the city walls. He is represented as a celestial monarch complete with a halo, signifying his divinity, and a mantle of imperial crimson connoting his sovereign power. Jesus' outstretched arms gather about him those ill in body and soul. They include a feeble elderly woman, a cripple holding crutches, a prisoner in shackles, a mother with a sick baby, and a woman clasping her head in despair. Their faces reflect pain and grief.

The scene is surrounded by an elaborate Renaissance-style aedicule, an architectural frame used in art to set off a representation of a deity. The aedicule is decorated with swags of fruit and laurel leaves, a traditional way of celebrating gods honored in such shrines. In the center of its broken pediment is a flaming urn, its fire representing the presence of the Holy Spirit. On the pediment slopes sit cherubs holding ewers, symbols of cleansing.

The base of the aedicule frames images of somewhat comical fish. A fish is one of the earliest symbols for Christians. Panels in the upper part of the aedicule display griffins, creatures with the head and wings of an eagle and the body of a lion. Griffins symbolize the dual nature of Christ: divine (bird) and human (animal). The griffins in this window may also refer to the person to whom the window is dedicated, Griffin B. Davenport, a Richmond merchant.

The maker of the window is not recorded in church records. Paul Norton, an authority on Gorham Studios stained glass, has attributed the window to the English firm, Heaton, Butler & Bayne, which used the Gorham Manufacturing Company as the firm's American agent.

ELLA DE TREVILLE WINDOW

TIFFANY STUDIOS
INSTALLED 1906

Dedicated to the memory of Ella de Treville (1845-1890)
Donated by Ella de Treville Snelling, daughter of Ella de Treville

THE ANGEL OF HOPE

The window terminating the church's east gallery is a glowing display of the special effects of Tiffany glass. Because the window faces south, and receives direct sun, its iridescent colors change in quality and intensity as light penetrates the various layers of glass at different times of the day. The distinctly opalescent character of Tiffany glass is particularly evident in the window's bottom panels, which indeed resemble deeply colored opals. Tiffany's ability to represent cloth in glass is well displayed in the angel's peach-colored robes. As with nearly all of the studios' windows, the angel's face is hand-painted, and is set off here by soulful eyes. The window is one of the three Tiffany works in the church to have a discernible signature, in this case a very discreet one in the lower right.

The subject is a single figure, the Angel of Hope, seen floating in an aspiring pose amid puffy blue clouds. The Angel of Hope represents a theological virtue, not an expectation of worldly reward through divine intervention. Hope's immediate object is God, the supreme expression of supernatural good. Hope, along with faith and charity, are the essential Christian verities. The Angel of Hope, while not Biblically referenced, has for centuries been a personification of the virtue of hope, an icon for those seeking divine grace and guidance. In this depiction, the angel reaches to embrace a star appearing in radiant light above. The five-pointed star, a symbol of divine guidance, has traditionally been used as a sign to ward off evil spirits, and in former times was frequently applied to thresholds and gates.

Ella Mitchell de Treville, who is memorialized here, was one of the first infants to be baptized in St. Paul's. Her father, William Mitchell, Jr., served on the church's building committee.

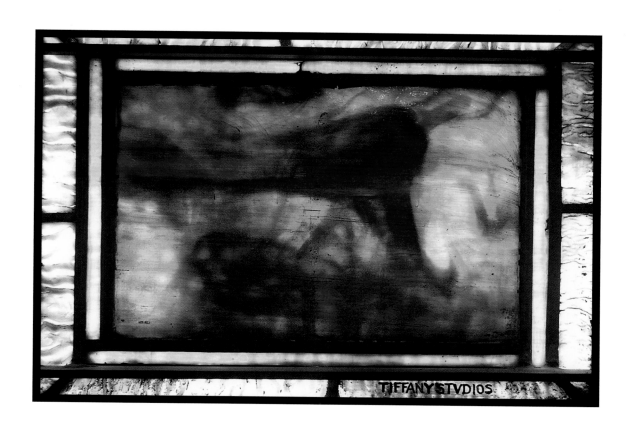

WILLIAM HAMILTON MACFARLAND WINDOW

ATTRIBUTED TO LAVERS & WESTLAKE
INSTALLED 1890

Dedicated to the memory of
William Hamilton Macfarland (1799-1872)
Donated by Nancy Macfarland, his widow, and their children

THE RESURRECTION

The Macfarland window is one of the set of four windows installed during the chancel enlargement of 1889-90. They portray different visions or aspects of Christ's life and being: the Epiphany, Resurrection, Ascension, and Christ the King. The Macfarland window depicts the Resurrection. Christ is seen as a dramatic revelation, still clothed in his burial shroud and hovering on clouds. Both hands of his outstretched arms reveal the Crucifixion nail prints in his palms, while with his right he makes the sign of the Trinity. The inscription reads: "Why Seek Ye The Living Among The Dead, He Is Not Here But Is Risen."

A remarkable feature of the scene is the surrounding mandorla, or light emanating from a divine being, usually shown as almond shaped. Here the mandorla is composed entirely of cherubim and seraphim, angels depicted as winged faces of infants. The outer ring consists of seraphim, traditionally colored red. The inner ring is of cherubim, normally represented in blue but also in gold, as here. Cherubim and seraphim are the highest ranked of the celestial hierarchy; their purpose is to proclaim the glory of God. The large number of angels' faces crowded about Jesus here may include as many as fifty.

Just below the clouds, and sitting on a ledge, are the two white-robed figures described by Luke as being at Jesus' empty tomb. One holds a palm branch, a Christian symbol of victory over death. The other raises his hand in telling that Jesus is no longer here. In the lower area are the three women named in Mark's version of the scene: Mary Magdalene, Mary the mother of James, and Salome. One holds the vessel of spices brought to anoint the body. Their expressions capture the instant between shock and joy.

The window honors William H. Macfarland, who served as a Virginia lieutenant governor and a member of the 1861 Virginia Convention ratifying secession from the Union. Macfarland served on the vestry for many years and also was senior warden.

ELIZABETH MAYO ROSS WINDOW

ATTRIBUTED TO LAVERS & WESTLAKE
INSTALLED 1890

Dedicated to the memory of Elizabeth Mayo Ross (1816-1874)
Donated by Judge Erskine Ross, son of Elizabeth Mayo Ross

THE ASCENSION

The four 1890 chancel windows, depicting different aspects of Christ, follow the medieval tradition of using windows as a way to help people, particularly those unable to read, comprehend Biblical stories and personalities. Stained-glass windows thus had the dual function of serving as teaching objects and works of art.

The subject of the Ross window is the Ascension. Jesus is shown lifted into Heaven on stormy clouds, his ascent guided by a host of angels. As with the Sarah Eliza Anderson window, Jesus is splendidly clothed. His cassock is imperial crimson, while his robe is a finely embroidered white cloth with a gold border. Jesus' hands are raised in blessing; his right hand makes the sign of the Trinity. The stigmata, or nail wounds in his palms, are clearly visible.

Below, a group watches the spectacle in wonder. Each of the six carefully painted male faces is circled by a halo. They likely depict Peter, John, James, Andrew, Philip, and Thomas, who are listed in the Book of Acts as the first disciples to return to Jerusalem following the Ascension. The story in Acts also includes the Virgin Mary, who is seen here draped in a blue robe. Blue, the color symbolic of Heaven, reminds us that Mary is the Queen of Heaven. The miraculous scene is proclaimed in the window's inscription: "And When He Had Spoken These Things While They Beheld, He Was Taken Up And A Cloud Received Him Out Of Their Sight."

The window was given by Judge Erskine Ross, a justice on the California Supreme Court, in memory of his mother, a St. Paul's parishioner. Judge Ross' brother, Dr. George Ross, was a long-time vestryman and senior warden of St. Paul's.

Joseph Reid Anderson Altarpiece

TIFFANY STUDIOS
INSTALLED 1896

Dedicated to the memory of Joseph Reid Anderson (1813-1892)
Donated by Mary Pegram Anderson, widow of Joseph Reid Anderson

The Last Supper

St. Paul's foremost work of art is the Tiffany Studios mosaic altarpiece, a reproduction of Leonardo da Vinci's fresco of the Last Supper. In addition to stained-glass windows, Tiffany Studios created notable religious objects in other materials, mosaic being a specialty. Leonardo's depiction of Jesus with his disciples in the upper room is among the world's most famous and admired artistic creations, capturing the moment immediately following Jesus' announcement that one of them would betray him. The startled disciples immediately lean among themselves, asking: "Is it I, Lord?"

In recent decades, reproductions of famous works of

art have been looked upon with some derision, particularly copies of such noted icons as Leonardo's Last Supper. We need to remember, however, that until the convenience of modern travel, and the invention of high resolution color photography, the only way most people, particularly Americans, could know and appreciate famous European works of art was through reproductions. In addition, by the late nineteenth century, Leonardo's fresco in Milan had seriously deteriorated. Tiffany's vividly colored depiction of this work, rendered not in tempera but in glass enamel with a background of gold, brought the work brilliantly alive for people who would otherwise never see it.

The altarpiece is the jewel of St. Paul's chancel, as

expanded to its present configuration in 1890. The installation of such a work of religious art is a reflection of the liturgical reforms brought about in the Anglican Communion as the result of the ecclesiological movement of the mid-nineteenth century. In St. Paul's, the original Protestant center-pulpit arrangement was swept away and replaced by an altar with flanking pulpit and lectern. The mosaic altarpiece was originally set in a dull gold frame. This was replaced by the current marble frame in 1913 when the present marble altar by Lamb Studios was given in memory of Mrs. Joseph Reid Anderson by her sister, Mrs. David G. McIntosh.

SARAH ELIZA ANDERSON WINDOW

ATTRIBUTED TO LAVERS & WESTLAKE
INSTALLED 1890

Dedicated to the memory of Sarah Eliza Anderson (1819-1881),
first wife of Joseph Reid Anderson
Donated by Joseph Reid Anderson

CHRIST THE KING

With its location in the center of the apse, immediately above the altar, the Sarah Eliza Anderson window is the focus of St. Paul's interior. Its subject is a stately image of the ascended Christ or Jesus transformed as *Christus Rex*— Christ the King. This regal figure is placed within a Renaissance arch, the pilasters of which are decorated with arabesques. Inscribed on the face of the arch is Jesus' blessing: "My Peace I Give Unto You." To underscore the message, Jesus' right hand is raised with his three fingers in the position of bestowing the Trinitarian benediction.

The front of the platform on which Jesus stands is decorated with floral swags containing red roses, symbols of his martyrdom. His death by crucifixion is evidenced by the stigmata or nail imprint on his left hand. By contrast, his royal status is signaled by his mantle of imperial crimson and by his golden crown. The crown is decorated with reliefs of cherubim, angels having only heads and wings. Embroidered on the breast, sleeve, and skirt of Jesus' white cassock is the monogram, IHS, the first three letters of the Greek version of the name of Jesus. IHS can also mean *In hoc signo* (in this sign).

Along with its companion apse windows, this window is in the style of Renaissance-period stained glass, characterized by strong clear colors contrasting with gold and buff hues that are highlighted with much painted decoration. The face of Christ is delicately delineated; his expression is at once both powerful and compassionate.

Sarah Eliza Anderson was the first wife of Joseph Reid Anderson, who is memorialized in the Tiffany window on the east aisle and in the altarpiece. Along with her husband, Mrs. Anderson was one of the original members of St. Paul's who transferred from Monumental Church. On the basis of its style and execution, Peter Cormack, acting keeper of the William Morris Gallery, London, has attributed the window to the London firm of Lavers & Westlake.

PEGRAM WINDOW

ATTRIBUTED TO LAVERS & WESTLAKE
INSTALLED 1890

*Dedicated to the memory of James West Pegram (1803-1844) and his wife, Virginia Johnson Pegram (1810-1888)
Donated by their daughter, Mary Pegram Anderson, second wife of Joseph Reid Anderson*

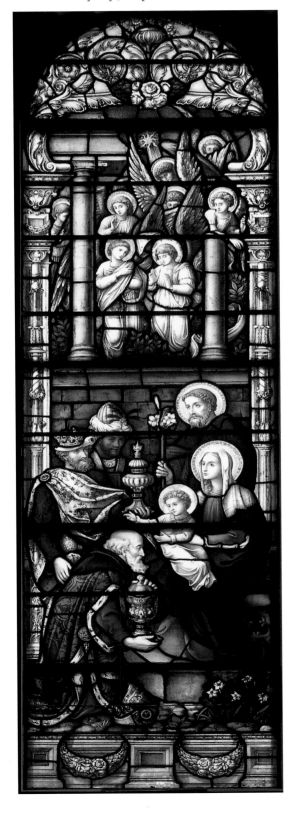

THE EPIPHANY

The visit of the Magi is a defining moment in Christian theology. Because the Magi were not Jews, this symbolic event conveys the fact that the infant Jesus was born not only to be the messiah of the Jews but also a revelation of God's grace to all people. The assumption that the wise men who came to honor the Christ child were three in number is based on the Matthew story of the Magi's three gifts. Their gifts—gold, frankincense, and myrrh—furthermore have important symbolism. Gold signals tribute to a monarch, for the wise men were seeking the King of the Jews; frankincense is incense traditionally burnt at altars, a sign of Jesus' divine nature; myrrh, an aromatic resin used for embalming, is an omen of Christ's martyrdom.

The window shows the Magi as splendidly dressed potentates; one even wears a crown. Their gifts are held in jeweled containers. Another of the three has a dark complexion, a reflection of the tradition that one of the Magi was African. As shown here, the Holy Family has the infant Jesus reaching to receive their offerings, thus acknowledging their meanings. Mary's purity is marked by the stalk of lilies in her hand. Above, a host of angels lends divine sanction to the event. Hovering over them is the star that guided the Magi. Typical of Renaissance-style windows, the rich colors employed here are highlighted by beautifully delineated painted decorations. The artistry of this work is evident especially in the Magi's expressive eyes and in the individual hairs of their beards. The maker of this and the other three 1890 chancel windows was not recorded in church records, but the windows have been attributed to Lavers & Westlake of London.

General James West Pegram, who is memorialized here, was one of the original contributors to the construction of St. Paul's Church. He was killed in a steamboat explosion on the Ohio River.

GEORGE WOODBRIDGE WINDOW

H.W. JENKINS & SON
DONATED IN 1879 TO MONUMENTAL CHURCH BY ITS CONGREGATION IN
MEMORY OF THE REV. GEORGE WOODBRIDGE, D.D. (1804-1878)

*Installed in St. Paul's in 1998 in memory of
Stepan Beducian (1887-1955) and his wife
Nazley Beducian (1895-1947),
and Jack Diradour (1888-1951) and his wife
Olivia Diradour (1889-1944)
Reinstallation donated by Mrs. Jeff Diradour and
Albert S. Diradour*

JESUS THE GOOD SHEPHERD

The west chancel window was originally installed in Monumental Church as a memorial to the Rev. George Woodbridge, its rector from 1845 until his death. The histories of Monumental Church and St. Paul's are closely linked. In 1845, the bulk of Monumental's congregation transferred to the newly completed St. Paul's Church. Monumental's rector, the Rev. William Norwood, resigned to become the first rector of St. Paul's. A few individuals preferred to remain at Monumental, and invited the Rev. George Woodbridge, rector of Christ Church "in the valley of this city," to bring his congregation to Monumental. The move was duly made and Monumental's parish was re-established.

The Monumental Church parish lasted until the 1960s, when it was disbanded. The building then became the property of the Medical College of Virginia Foundation. Monumental eventually was acquired by the Historic Richmond Foundation, which continued the restoration begun by the MCV Foundation around 1970. The project included removing the memorial windows and replacing them with replicas of the original clear-glass windows.

The Woodbridge window is a classic example of Victorian stained glass, being dominated by rich, clear colors composing a bold but sentimental pictorial image. The scene is Jesus as the good shepherd, a portrayal of the window's inscription: "Feed My Lambs." Jesus is shown amid a flock of sheep, holding a shepherd's crook in one hand and tenderly cradling a lamb with the other. The scene is framed by a Gothic tabernacle, elaborately decorated with crockets and finials.

A *Richmond Dispatch* account of January 27, 1879 states that the window was made by H. W. Jenkins & Son of Baltimore, with Mr. E. L. Young superintending the work. The Diradours and Beducians emigrated from Turkey, and became attached to St. Paul's when it accommodated services for the Armenian community.

JOHN MARSHALL WINDOW

LAMB STUDIOS
DONATED IN 1901 TO MONUMENTAL CHURCH IN MEMORY OF
JOHN MARSHALL (1755-1835)

Installed in St. Paul's in 1998 in memory of
Dabney Stewart Lancaster (1889-1975) and his wife
Mary Tabb Crump Lancaster (1889-1984), and
Judge Beverley T. Crump (1854-1930)
and his wife Henrietta Tayloe Crump (1861-1949)
Reinstallation donated by Mr. and Mrs. H. Merrill Pasco

MOSES PRESENTING THE TEN COMMANDMENTS

This representation of Moses with the tablets of the Ten Commandments was originally placed in Richmond's Monumental Church as a memorial to U. S. Chief Justice John Marshall, one of that church's founding members. As part of the Historic Richmond Foundation's long-term restoration of Monumental Church to its original appearance, the Marshall window, along with five other late 19th-century stained-glass windows, was removed in 1996. The six windows were divided between St. Paul's and St. James's churches. The three windows received by St. Paul's were restored and slightly modified to fit where the former organ was located. Side panels belonging to each window could not be reused, but have been preserved by the parish.

The window's subject alludes to John Marshall, the nation's most famed chief justice, whose interpretations of the United States Constitution established significant legal precedents. Like Moses, Marshall was a lawgiver to an emerging nation. Moses is depicted here much as popular imagination has represented him over the centuries. He is a stern and imposing patriarchal figure with a long beard and piercing eyes. The Ten Commandments are inscribed in Hebrew on the pair of stone tablets. The Commandments served as a form of constitution by which the Jews would relate to Yahweh and establish their nation once they entered the Promised Land. Behind Moses is the barren mountainous landscape of the Sinai Peninsula where he and his followers wandered for forty years.

Judge Beverley T. Crump served on St. Paul's vestry and was a strong supporter of St. Paul's Church Home for Young Girls. Dabney S. Lancaster was state superintendent of public instruction and served on the boards of trustees of several educational institutions including Virginia Theological Seminary.

John Brockenbrough Newton Window

TIFFANY STUDIOS
DONATED IN 1899 TO MONUMENTAL CHURCH BY ITS CONGREGATION IN
MEMORY OF
THE RIGHT REVEREND JOHN BROCKENBROUGH NEWTON (1839-1897)

*Installed in St. Paul's in 1998 in memory of
John Henry Guy (1878-1953) and
Katherine Lancaster Guy (1886-1978)
Reinstallation donated by Mr. and Mrs. Briscoe Guy
and descendants of Bishop Newton*

CHRIST'S ASCENSION

This arresting visualization of Christ ascending to Heaven by the Tiffany Studios was originally created for Monumental Church as a memorial to John Brockenbrough Newton, rector of that church from 1884 to 1894. Newton was trained as a physician but became an ordained minister after serving as a Confederate surgeon. From 1894 to 1897, he was bishop coadjutor of the Diocese of Virginia. His death on Ascension Day 1897, provided the inspiration for the window's subject. According to Monumental Church records, the window is the work of Frederick Wilson of the Tiffany Company, also known as Tiffany Studios. The original side panels were not reused when the window was installed, but are owned by St. Paul's.

The Newton window is characteristic of the Tiffany style, with subtle, misty tones obtained with the use of translucent layered glass. The composition's sinuous movement is emphasized by the many elongated pieces of drapery glass used in the garments of the various figures. The colors range from dark and rich in the lower figures to light and luminescent in Christ's garment and in the aerial portions of the upper section. Centered in the group below is the Virgin Mary in her traditional blue robe. She is placed among the Apostles, whose faces display grave looks of awe as they watch Jesus being lifted into Heaven on the wings of flanking angels. Because the Newton and the other two Monumental Church windows are not on an outside wall, they are artificially lighted.

Katherine Lancaster Guy, in whose memory the window was reinstalled in St. Paul's, served as the first president of the earliest St. Catherine's School Alumnae Association and was a president of the Women's Auxiliary of the Episcopal Diocese of Virginia.

HAXALL WINDOW

CHARLES BOOTH STUDIO
INSTALLED 1892

Dedicated to the memory of Bolling Walker Haxall (1814-1885)
and
Anne Triplett Haxall (1820-1889)
Donated by their children: Triplett Haxall, Mrs. Charles Harrison,
and Bolling Haxall

JESUS AMONG THE ELDERS

Charles Booth, designer of the Haxall window, maintained a stained-glass business in London, but also worked for a time in New Jersey, where he was represented by an agent in New York City. He produced numerous windows for both English and American churches, including a window for Richmond's historic St. John's Church.

The Haxall window, designed the year before Booth's death in 1893, and probably executed by his New Jersey studio, is an exceptional example of Victorian art. It depicts the young Jesus among the temple elders, as told in Luke's Gospel. The composition is based on a famous painting of the same subject by the 19th-century German artist, Heinrich Hofmann. The figures flanking Jesus are near replicas of those in Hofmann's work. The execution of the two elders immediately to the right of Jesus is a tour-de-force of stained-glass painting. The handling of their keen expressions, particularly the delineation of their skin and beards, recalls the precision draftsmanship in an Albrecht Dürer painting.

The focal point of the scene is the boy Jesus, standing confidently on the temple steps where he astounds the scholarly elders and teachers with his questions and understanding of scripture. One of the elders holds a manuscript of Hebrew writings, using it as a reference for the dialogue; the others ponder Jesus' every word. The window's inscription: "And They Shall See His Face And His Name Shall Be In Their Foreheads" reflects the importance of Jesus' first visit to the temple.

Jesus' white garment symbolizes youthful purity. The nimbus or luminescence surrounding his head signals his sanctity. The elegant pendant cornice above Jesus reminds us that the setting is the Jerusalem temple, epicenter of the Jewish faith. The grandeur of the architecture is emphasized by the columned apse in the background.

Strother-Buford Window

TIFFANY STUDIOS
INSTALLED 1916

*Dedicated to the memory of
Mary Cameron Ross Buford (1848-1916) and her husbands,
Robert Quarles Strother (1844-1873) and
Algernon Sidney Buford (1826-1911)
Donated by Elisabeth Strother Scott, daughter of Mr. and Mrs.
Robert Strother, and step-daughter of Algernon Sidney Buford*

The Kiss of Charity

A work of singular beauty, the Strother-Buford window displays all the creativity and aesthetic vitality of Tiffany stained glass. The design is a visual representation of the window's inscription: "Greet Ye One Another With a Kiss Of Charity," (1 Peter 5: 14). The kiss of charity is a symbol of love and affection. In Christian practice such a kiss is a way of expressing faithfulness and forgiveness, and of saying that two people harbor no enmity.

Greeting with a holy kiss was a common practice in the early Church, acknowledging that believers were one in the Lord. The innocence and purity of the kiss of charity is visually expressed here through two young children, with the blessing of a motherly figure who rests her hands on them. The small girl holds a bouquet of white flowers, also a symbol of purity. Despite the effort to illustrate the innocence of the act, the facial expressions of the two children can only be described as sensual.

The representational qualities of Tiffany's work are seen especially in the treatment of the architectural elements. The opalescent glass used to depict the Ionic pilasters, shell niche, and side panels conveys the impression of fine marble. Tiffany's mastery of flowers, so evident in Tiffany lampshades, is beautifully illustrated in the clusters of morning glories spilling over the edge of the walls. The garden-like scene is highlighted with a backdrop of Italian cypress trees through which shines a pink sunrise sky. The window is signed "Tiffany Studio, 1916" at the bottom left.

Elisabeth Strother Scott, the window's donor, was married to Frederic William Scott, a founder of the Richmond brokerage firm of Scott and Stringfellow. The Scotts' children and grandchildren have contributed significantly to the life of St. Paul's parish; many have served on the vestry over the years.

JEFFERSON DAVIS WINDOW (LOWER)

TIFFANY STUDIOS
INSTALLED 1898

Dedicated to the memory of Jefferson Davis (1808-1889),
President of the Confederate States of America
Donated by general subscription

PAUL BEFORE HEROD AGRIPPA

St. Paul's most famous windows are the pair honoring Jefferson Davis. The idea of a window perpetuating the memory of the church's renowned member was first discussed by a vestry committee in 1889, the year of Davis' death. The project remained in abeyance until 1896, when Mrs. George Ross's committee of ladies raised sufficient funds to commission the window. The Tiffany Studios sent sketches for both the upper and lower windows the following year.

The subject chosen for the lower window was St. Paul before King Herod Agrippa. As recounted in the Book of Acts, Paul, a Roman citizen, had been imprisoned for two years, but a newly appointed procurator, Pontius Festus, determined he was being held on insufficient grounds. When Herod Agrippa learned this, he asked that Paul be brought to him to explain Christian doctrines. The window captures this dramatic incident. Chained to a soldier, Paul stands before the pondering king and his sister Bernice. The ghostly figure of Festus stands beside the king. Paul tells of his conversion and of his charge to spread the gospel. Herod Agrippa confesses he is almost convinced. He admits that he

JEFFERSON DAVIS

would have freed Paul had Paul not already appealed his case to Caesar. He thus sent Paul to Rome for trial.

This Biblical event alludes to Jefferson Davis's own two-year imprisonment following the Civil War, an incarceration that most Southerners felt was unjust. Like Paul, Davis was held in chains, and though both sought to plead their case in court, neither stood trial, and both were released on bond.

Davis's effort to obtain justice is emphasized by the window's inscription: "This Man Doeth Nothing Worthy of Death or Bonds" (Acts 26: 31).

The window, the work of Tiffany's artisan, Frederick Wilson, was unveiled with great solemnity at a special afternoon service on Easter Sunday, April 17, 1898. It likely is no coincidence that Wilson's image of St. Paul is reminiscent of Jefferson Davis.

Jefferson Davis Window (upper)

Tiffany Studios
Installed 1898

Dedicated to the memory of Jefferson Davis (1808-1889),
President of the
Confederate States of America
Donated by general subscription

The Angels of Goodness and Mercy

The upper section of the pair of windows honoring Jefferson Davis is a dramatic component of this famous memorial. It contrasts with the lower window, which is a representation of a specific historic event, and which lacks the mystical imagery typically seen in Tiffany's religious works. This mystical quality, however, is vividly present in the upper section and lends spiritual sanction to the scene below.

The upper window also served as a vehicle for expressing strongly felt contemporary attitudes about Jefferson Davis' character. Southern loyalists, including members of Davis' own parish of St. Paul's, held that Davis had been cruelly and unjustly treated with his arrest and imprisonment following the defeat of the Confederacy. They regarded Davis as a man of noble fiber, who led his people in a virtuous cause against invaders. Like St. Paul, he was considered wrongly accused. This window thus has as its inscription: "Let Me Be Weighed In An Even Balance That God May Know Mine Integrity." (Job 31:6). Expressing this theme, the window portrays the angels of goodness and mercy, whose downcast eyes subliminally convey a message that Davis merits their attributes. More specifically, they are symbolic emblems of the sixth verse of the twenty-third Psalm: "Surely goodness and mercy shall follow me all the days of my life and I will dwell in the house of the Lord forever."

Both the composition and the execution of the window are quintessentially Tiffany. Swirls of luminous glass form the angels' radiant robes and uplifted wings. Ribbon glass, or glass with actual drapery-like folds, is used abundantly in the garments. The notion of purity is expressed in the white lilies cradled in the angel's arm. Emphasizing the scene's ethereal quality are the flaming torches held by each figure, the smoke from which spirals up through the angels' wings. Though not mentioned in contemporary descriptions, the torches here likely symbolize the light of truth.

CHARLES MACGILL WINDOW

Dedicated to the memory of Charles Macgill, M.D. (1806-1881)
Donated by Mary Macgill, widow of Dr. Macgill

JESUS RAISING THE YOUNG MAN AT NAIN

Silas McBee, who designed both Macgill windows, was an Episcopal educator, writer, and architect. In addition to working as a stained-glass artist, McBee served as editor of *The Churchman*, and was founder and editor of *Constructive Quarterly*. In 1894, while engaged as a liturgical consultant for Grace Parish, Galveston, Texas, one of its parishioners, Mrs. Henry Rosenberg, asked McBee to provide drawings for a window in St. Paul's honoring Dr. Charles Macgill, her father. The window was duly crafted to McBee's design by the studio of Charles Booth, which continued operation in Orange, New Jersey, though Booth had died in 1893.

The window's subject is Jesus raising the young man at Nain. As told in the seventh chapter of Luke, Jesus arrived at the city gate where a dead man, the only son of his widowed mother, was being brought out for burial. A crowd from the city followed in procession. Having compassion for the grief-stricken mother, Jesus touched the bier and told the young man to arise, whereupon he sat up and began to speak. The young man, draped in his funeral shroud and just awakened from death, stares at Jesus, whose hand remains outstretched. His speechless mother is wearing a purple mantle, its color signifying human devotion. Behind her, the accompanying crowd looks on in astonishment. In the background we can see sections of the city of Nain among the hills.

Charles Macgill began his medical practice in Maryland, where he continued until 1861, when he was arrested and imprisoned by Federals as a Southern sympathizer. Confederate troops released him following their invasion of Maryland the next year. Dr. Macgill then came to Virginia, where President Jefferson Davis appointed him a military surgeon, an office he held for the duration of the Civil War. He became a member of St. Paul's and was confirmed here.

MACGILL-SWAN WINDOW

SILAS MCBEE, DESIGNER
CHARLES BOOTH STUDIO, MAKER
INSTALLED 1896

Dedicated to the memory of Ellen E. Swan (1830-1890),
Richard Ragan Macgill (1831-1860),
William D. Macgill (1835-1889), and
Clara Macgill (1842-1851)
Donated by their mother, Mary Macgill (1807-1897),
widow of Charles Macgill, M. D.

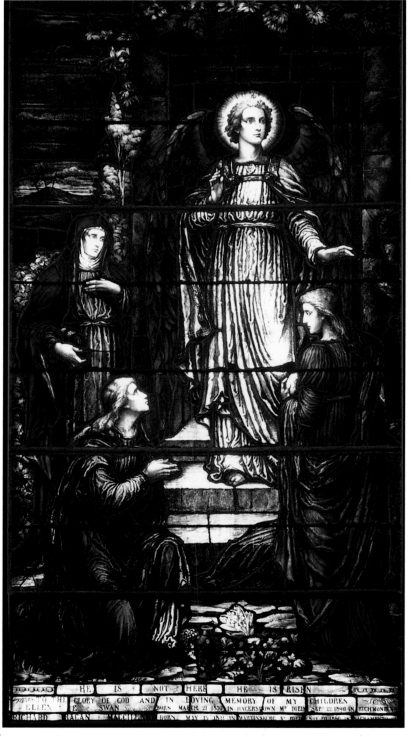

THE WOMEN AT THE TOMB

The Macgill-Swan window memorializes Mary Macgill's four children who preceded her in death. Like its companion window, honoring Mrs. Macgill's husband, it was designed by Silas McBee, and executed by Charles Booth's studio. Mrs. Macgill apparently died soon after its dedication, since a surviving daughter, Mrs. Henry Rosenberg, wrote the vestry in 1897 asking permission to install a window in memory of her mother next to her father's window. The vestry, however, adopted a policy of allowing no more windows for private memorials. The policy was not maintained since several memorial windows were subsequently installed.

To counter its somber genesis, Mrs. Macgill agreed that the subject for the window in memory of her children would be a scene from the Resurrection. McBee chose Mark's account for his depiction. The number of women at the tomb varies in each Gospel. Mark's mentions three: Mary Magdalene, Mary, mother of James, and Salome. Following the Sabbath, the three women came to the tomb to anoint Jesus' body with spices. Upon arrival, they found the entrance stone rolled away. In the tomb was a young man dressed in white, who tells them that Jesus is not there, but has risen from the dead. The window elaborates on the scene by having the young man depicted as an angel with red wings and a golden cape. His face, with its finely chiseled features, is highlighted by an aureole, or circle of light, indicating he is a holy personage.

In the upper left of the background is the barren hillside of Calvary with three empty crosses silhouetted against a stormy sky. Lying among the flowers along the bottom of the window is a jeweled spice vessel, dropped by one of the women in her astonishment.

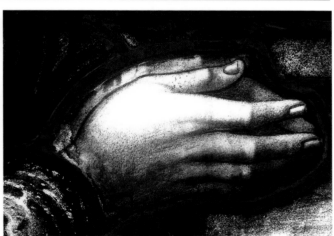

RICHARD L. MAURY AND MATTHEW F. MAURY WINDOW

GORHAM MANUFACTURING COMPANY
INSTALLED 1910

Dedicated to the memory of
Richard Launcelot Maury (1840-1907) and his son
Matthew Fontaine Maury II (1863-1908)
Donated by Susan E. Maury, widow of Richard L. Maury

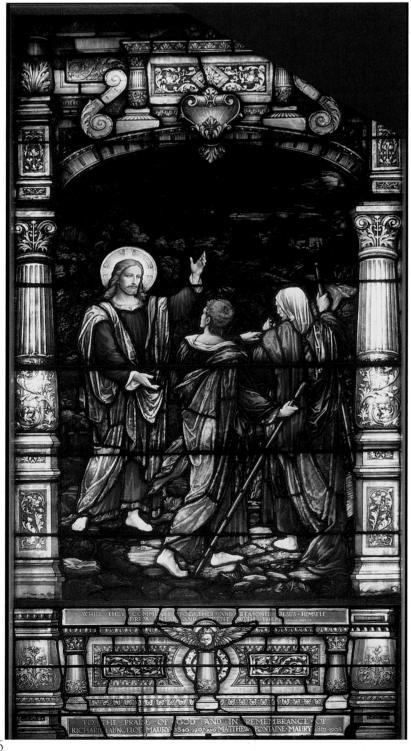

JESUS ON THE ROAD TO EMMAUS

The two parishioners to whom this richly detailed window is dedicated were the son and grandson of Commodore Matthew Fontaine Maury, the famous oceanographer, known to history as "Pathfinder of the Seas." Like many of his fellow churchgoers Richard Launcelot Maury was a Confederate veteran, having served as a colonel in the 24th Virginia regiment. Col. Maury was also one of the incorporators of the St. Paul's Endowment Fund in 1905, established to provide for the preservation of the church should the parish suffer significant membership loss. The endowment's value has increased substantially and is used today for the upkeep of the church and to support many charitable causes.

The subject of the Maury window is Jesus on the way to Emmaus. This incident, recorded in Luke's gospel, tells that on the day after the Resurrection, two of the apostles were walking to Emmaus when Jesus suddenly appeared and walked with them. Only after they arrived at the village and broke bread with Jesus did they realize that he was their risen Lord. This story was meant to convey that death could not contain the meaning and power of Jesus' being. For the Maury family it also signified that a father and son, who died only nine weeks apart, could be reunited in the presence of Jesus Christ.

In the window, we see Jesus appearing to the two apostles as they walk on the rocky way to Emmaus. We know the name of only one of them, Cleopas. Though startled, they are about to tell Jesus, whom they do not recognize, that he must be the only person unaware that their lord had been crucified, and that there was rumor of his resurrection. This profound moment is depicted here in jewel-like richness. Like the Maury window above, the scene is surrounded by an elaborate architectural frame, giving it the character of a holy icon.

COMMUNED · TOGETHER · AND · REASONED,
DREW · NEAR, AND · WENT · WITH · THE

SUSAN E. MAURY WINDOW

GORHAM MANUFACTURING COMPANY
INSTALLED 1912

Dedicated to the memory of Susan Elizabeth Maury (1841-1911),
widow of Richard Launcelot Maury (1840-1907)
Donated by their daughter, Anne H. Maury

THE ANGEL OF PEACE

Susan E. Maury died just one year after the dedication of the window she donated in memory of her husband and her son. Her daughter, Anne H. Maury, thus determined to present a window honoring her deceased mother. It was decided to locate it immediately above the first Maury window, and to have it also crafted by the Gorham Company. The vestry stated its desire that the window be consistent with the rest of the windows in the upper west gallery, and not be too dark so as to avoid darkening the church interior. In a subsequent meeting, the vestry requested that the window be installed on a pivot so it could be opened in warm weather.

As with several other upper-gallery windows, the upper Maury window is not based on a specific Biblical event, but is a visual personification of the window's inscription, taken from Psalm 29: "The Lord Will Bless His People With Peace." Accordingly, the central figure is an angel of peace descending to earth on the rays of Heaven. The word "angel" means a messenger—a bringer of tidings. The angel has ruby-red wings and holds an olive branch, a symbol of peace. Olive leaves are also seen in the angel's hair.

Accompanying the angel are several cherubim and seraphim, angels having only heads and wings. Both orders of angels are usually shown with heads of infants. Cherubim are traditionally depicted with blue wings, seraphim with red. Their faces here are especially endearing. This fantastic vision of divine visitation is set in an elaborate aedicule or shrine-type architectural frame composed here of Corinthian columns supporting a stone arch with a heavily decorated lintel. The base of the frame is likewise encrusted with architectural motifs.

The Gorham Manufacturing Company, best know for its silver products, produced stained-glass windows through its American Window Department from 1904 into the early 1920s.

Marie and Kate Gerdy Window

Franz Mayer Co., Munich
Installed 1936

*Dedicated to the memory of Marie Gerdy (died 1934)
and her sister, Kate Gerdy (died 1932, age 77)*

The Gerdy window, honoring two of the parish's faithful communicants, is the left window of the chapel's three Franz Mayer works installed in the 1930s. The window is signed "F. Mayer Munich." Like its companions, its style is closely patterned after the famous medieval windows in Chartres Cathedral. A conspicuous aspect of the Chartres examples, reproduced here, is the mosaic effect resulting from hundreds of small bits of glass in clear primary colors. The dominant hues are ruby reds, ambers, and sapphire blues. Another characteristic of such medieval glass is the multiplicity of stylized Biblical scenes and figures woven into the overall composition.

The principal scene of this window, the Nativity, is framed by the middle quatrefoil. Here we see Mary and Joseph watching over the infant Jesus wrapped in his swaddling clothes. The heads of the cow and donkey peering over a fence remind us of the humble stable setting of Jesus' birth. In the panel above is another quatrefoil, framing a depiction of the angel telling the shepherds the news of the Navitity. Three sheep witness the event. The shepherds, grasping their crooks, stare up in wonder at the angel.

On the window's right side are vignette scenes of the three wise men. The upper vignette is of a dark-complexioned wise man holding his gift in an elegant container. His camel is behind him. Below are the two other wise men. One wears a crown, a symbol of his lofty status. Vignettes on the window's left side show additional shepherds. Connecting the various scenes is a lattice-like pattern of red diagonal struts against a blue background, a pattern also found in the Chartres windows.

In the window's lower section are two angels bearing a pillow on which rests a crown, a reminder of Jesus' royal divinity. Above the crown is a cross, a signal of Jesus' eventual crucifixion.

FANNY BRAXTON YOUNG WINDOW

FRANZ MAYER CO., MUNICH
INSTALLED 1937

Dedicated to the memory of Fanny Braxton Young Miller
(1859-1914), wife of
James Mason Miller
Donated by Fanny Braxton Williams and Margaret
Erskine Hutcheson, daughters of Fanny and James Miller

The Fanny Braxton Young window is the middle of the three Franz Mayer works installed in St. Paul's undercroft chapel in the 1930s. The Franz Mayer Co. is an architectural decoration firm founded in 1847 in Munich, Bavaria. It began producing stained glass around 1862, and continues to operate in family ownership.

As with the other two chapel windows, the Young window echoes the character of the celebrated medieval stained glass of Chartres Cathedral. Its mosaic-like quality is dominated by blues, reds and ambers. Worked into its complex patterns are images of Biblical events and figures. The window's focal point is the center section, a quatrefoil framing a representation of the Holy Family's flight into Egypt, as related in the Gospel of Matthew. Here we see Mary on a donkey holding the infant Jesus, with Joseph by their side. They are fleeing Judea to escape King Herod's intent to kill

all male children in the vicinity of Bethlehem.

The upper-section quatrefoil frames another Biblical story of Jesus' infancy: the visit to the temple in Jerusalem for the requisite offering of a sacrifice. As told in the Gospel of Luke, Mary is shown presenting the infant Jesus to Simeon, an elderly righteous man to whom God revealed that he would not die before seeing the Messiah. Cradling the infant in his arms, Simeon uttered the famous canticle, the *Nunc Dimittis*, in which he proclaimed that he has seen God's salvation. Joseph kneels opposite Mary, holding a caged pair of turtledoves, the sacrificial offering dictated by the law of Moses.

In the lower section is an image of Jesus as a young boy being venerated by two angels. The divinity of Jesus is expressed by the halo framing his head, and by his arms outstretched in a gesture of benediction. Jesus is also shown here standing on a globe, a signal of his pending role as Savior of the world.

MARIE COOKE HICKEY AND JAMES J. HICKEY WINDOW

FRANZ MAYER CO., MUNICH
INSTALLED 1937

Dedicated to the memory of Marie Cooke Hickey
(1872-1931) and
James J. Hickey (1873-1933)
Donated by St. Hilda's Guild

The right-hand chapel window honors Marie Cooke Hickey and her husband James J. Hickey, who made the restoration of the chapel possible. Mr. Hickey is also remembered for a generous thank offering, given by him for the purpose of ministering to the needs of widows and orphans of the clergy. The window is signed at the bottom right "F. Mayer Munich."

As with its companion Franz Mayer windows, the Hickey window is a rich texture of jewel-like patterns inter-

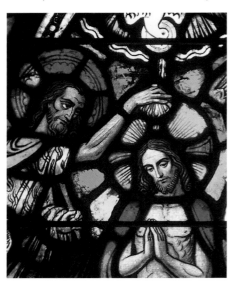

woven with stylized Biblical scenes and figures. The Mayer windows reflect the tradition of medieval stained glass to convey messages and stories while also being works of art. The Hickey window's central image is the baptism of Jesus. The scene, framed within a quatrefoil, shows John the Baptist performing the ritualistic cleansing of sins with the water of Jordan. The act is witnessed by an angel on Jesus' left. Above Jesus is a radiant dove, the personification of the Holy Spirit, which proclaimed Jesus to be God's beloved son.

The scene within the upper-section quatrefoil is of the twelve-year-old Jesus sitting among the elders in the Temple. In Luke's Gospel we are told that Jesus amazed the elders and teachers by his understanding of their answers to his questions. Jesus is seen here holding a book, a symbol of his grasp of the sacred texts. This symbolic event signaled Jesus' earliest awareness of his unique role. It was here that he told Mary that she should have been aware that the Temple was his Father's house.

In the window's lower panel is a depiction of the *Agnus Dei* or Lamb of God. This alludes to Jesus as the symbolic paschal or sacrificial lamb, one who gave himself as a sacrifice for the sins of the world. As is traditional with such representations, the lamb is shown holding a flag displaying a cross, the banner of the Resurrection.

Acknowledgments

The Book Committee members are Lyons Burke, Lois Biddison, Mary Holly Bigelow, Yvonne Gold, Myfanwy Hall, Calder Loth, Cyane Lowden and Claire Mills. The committee extends special thanks to the following for generously lending their expertise on stained glass: Peter Cormack, Acting Keeper, William Morris Gallery, London, for attributing the chancel windows to Lavers & Westlake; Paul Norton, Professor Emeritus, University of Massachusetts, for providing information on the American Window Department of the Gorham Manufacturing Company and related stained-glass artisans, and for attributing the Griffin B. Davenport window to Heaton, Butler & Bayne; Julie Sloan, stained glass consultant, North Adams, Massachusetts, for providing information on Charles Booth and other American stained-glass makers; and Donald Traser, Richmond historian, for sharing his invaluable early newspaper clippings and other information relating to the windows of St. Paul's and Monumental Church.

The committee thanks the following St. Paul's parishioners and friends for kindly proofreading the text: Lynn Bayliss, Alan Biddison, Sr., Earle Dunford, Lynn Evans, Anne Hobson Freeman, Peter Hodson, Philip Schwarz, and Liz Whitehurst.

Special appreciation is offered to Alton Ayer, property committee chairman, for his interest in this project and for directing the on-going conservation program for the windows.

Lastly, the committee thanks S. Buford Scott for serving as honorary fund-raising chairman for this book.

Information on the windows in this work is taken primarily from *St. Paul's Church Richmond, Virginia, Its Historic Years and Memorials*, by Elizabeth Wright Weddell (William Byrd Press, 1931), St. Paul's Vestry Minutes (on deposit in the Virginia Historical Society) and various Richmond newspaper clippings provided by Donald Traser and the Historic Richmond Foundation (photocopies on deposit in the St. Paul's Archives).

SPONSORS

Ernest Clifford Barrett, III in memory of Barbara Haxall Grundy Barrett

Mr. and Mrs. Frederic Scott Bocock

Lyons and George Burke in memory of Mary Simkins Taliaferro and Isham Trotter Hardy

Elisabeth Ross Reed Carter

Mrs. Elmuset B. Diradour in memory of Jeff Diradour

Episcopal Church Women of St. Paul's

Yvonne Gold in memory of Edouard Nies-Berger

Briscoe B. Guy in memory of Katherine Lancaster and John H. Guy

James H. Hall in memory of The Rev. Dr. J. Herrick Hall

Emily P. Kinnier in memory of Janet P. Nunnally, Elizabeth K. Bott, and Eugene H. Kinnier

Calder Loth in memory of Frances Alice Rust Loth

Virginia B. Maloney in memory of Frank C. Maloney, III

Dr. and Mrs. Hunter McGuire, Jr.

Ellen Boyd and William Read Miller in memory of Mary Todd and Robert Cammacle Duval,
Cecil Boyd Todd, Lucy Witt and John Littlepage Ingram, and the Hagner Family

Deane Hotchkiss Mountcastle in memory of Sallie Deane Carrington, Judith C. Arrington, and
R. Turner Arrington, Jr.

Property Committee of St. Paul's

David R. Ritter in memory of Irvin John Kendig Ritter and
in honor of Margaret Ann Stewart Ritter

Anna Lou and Bob Schaberg

Mrs. Frederic W. Scott in memory of Mr. Frederic W. Scott

The John Wingfield Scott Memorial Fund

Susie and Buford Scott

Mary Blair Scott Valentine in honor of Stuart Valentine

Jean and David White in memory of Hattie C. Clifton

Courtenay S. Wilson in memory of Courtenay and Jack Sands

Mary Denny Wray in memory of Mr. and Mrs. Frederic William Scott